Atlanta

A PHOTOGRAPHIC PORTRAIT

Photography by Byron Jorjorian

First published in the United States
of America by:

Twin Lights Publishers, Inc.
10 Hale Street
Rockport, Massachusetts 01966
Telephone: (978) 546-7398
http://www.twinlightspub.com

ISBN-13: 978-1-885435-58-4
ISBN-10: 1-885435-58-4

10 9 8 7 6 5 4 3 2 1

Editorial by Priscilla Morris

Book design by
SYP Design & Production, Inc.
http://www.sypdesign.com

Printed in China

INTRODUCTION

"Atlanta is always reinventing itself. It's never satisfied to stand still."

—Sam Williams, President, Metro Atlanta Chamber of Commerce

If you set out to find a place with a warmly temperate annual climate, a place with attitude, water views, natural beauty, metropolitan amenities, cozy neighborhoods and high culture—all within a two-hour flight of 80% of the nation's population—that place would be Atlanta, the dazzlingly busy capital of the new south. Atlanta is young: in 1837 it was a frontier rail hub that sprang from the Georgia piedmont near the Chattahoochee River. Atlanta is resilient: from Civil War to civil rights, the city has channeled the energy of tempestuous times to rebuild, to improve, to modernize.

As a commercial center, Atlanta still owes much to its roots in transport. It remains a busy rail and airfreight hub and has become a nerve center for media and information. UPS, Home Depot, and CNN are hometown companies. The city is the polestar of the "Boston to Austin" technology corridor. Long a land of opportunity for African-American businesses, immigrants from around the world are flocking to the area along with over 400 international companies. Atlanta has always entertained international aspirations; the 1996 Centennial Olympiad landed it squarely on the global stage. Growing diversity and international stature are fueling a boom in conference business, tourism, and sophisticated restaurant choices.

Metropolitan Atlanta is huge; over four million persons live in a 22-county area that now reaches all the way to Alabama. Amazingly, Atlanta has more forest cover than any other urban area in the country. From dogwood and magnolia to oaks and maples, activist organizations such as Trees Atlanta have imbued Atlanta with an appreciation for lush urban forest canopy. The city is distinguished by an excellent parks system, the Chattahoochee River National Recreation Area, Stone Mountain and its park, Kennesaw Mountain and its memorial, and hundreds of leafy, yet distinctive, neighborhoods. The abundance of natural elements, so valued and laced into the urban fabric, lend human scale to life in our ninth largest metropolis.

Our aim is for you to experience in these photographs the genetic code of Atlanta—trees, transport, transformation in the face of adversity. Despite its contemporary character, the city has preserved many of its heritage sites for interpretation or adaptive reuse. In these pages Byron Jorjorian examines a cross section of Atlanta's landmarks, trademarks, and hidden delights using aerials, abstracts, close-ups and his internationally acclaimed eye for the natural environment. His beautifully made photographs encapsulate the essence of Georgia's dynamic capital city today. This city is always changing; we hope these pages inspire you to document your own slice of the Big Peach.

▲ **Woodruff Arts Center**

Multi-institutional Woodruff Arts Center is the nexus for visual and performing arts in the heart of midtown. The complex provides testimony of Atlanta's sprit of renewal. It was built in tribute to 132 city arts leaders lost in a tragic plane crash in Orly, France in 1962. Responding to its great loss, the city rallied by funding this nationally respected campus for creative discovery.

▶ **Rhodes Hall at 100**

The castle on Peachtree Street was built a century ago by Amos Rhodes of Rhodes Furniture fame. It is the last remnant of a streetscape once lined by baronial estates built from Stone Mountain Granite. Rhodes Hall is available for grand occasions set in a peerless Romanesque-Revival mansion.

▲ **Spaghetti Junction**

If you live in Atlanta, it's no secret—the city is all about traffic. Planning a route and knowing the best time of day to get around town is a competitive sport around here. A twice-daily trip through Spaghetti Junction can be the deciding factor in whether to live in-town or OTP (outside the perimeter).

▶ **City of Traffic; City of Trees**

Boasting a skyline that stretches for miles, Atlanta is also known for its parks, greenspaces, and resplendent tree canopy.

▲ House of the People

The gold dome of the Georgia Capitol
Building as seen from the Westin
Peachtree Plaza—the tallest hotel in
the Western Hemisphere. Taking in the
360-degree view from the revolving
rooftop restaurant is a favorite way to get
oriented to the New York of the South.

▶ Postmodern Beauty

Many of Atlanta's world-class skyscrapers
were built in the 1990's. Award-winning
Peachtree Tower exemplifies the aspirations of a city continually raising its stan-
dards and reinventing itself. The building
culminates in the gracefully arched and
domed tower with twin crowns.

▲ **Light Painting**

Atlantans will never concede that traffic can be a beautiful thing, yet the serpentine infrastructure moving millions through the heart of the city is a marvel of engineering. Viewed from the air at night, the speed and motion is glorious.

◀ **Night Lights in Hotlanta**

The vibrancy and glow of this 24-hour city intensify at night. Midtown is awash with color as cars speed on and off the interstate for a slice of the Big Peach.

▲ Fountain of Rings

Centennial Olympic Park viewed from high atop the Westin Peachtree Plaza. Music emanates from speaker towers while lights and water shoot up from the five rings of the giant interactive fountain.

▶ The Pencil Building

The spire at the top of the Bank of America building is covered in 24-karat gold, casting a magnificent glow from sunlight and nighttime illumination. Shaped like a 1000 foot pencil, this spectacular 1992 addition to the skyline is one of the tallest buildings in the world.

▲ **Vertical Landscape from the Westin**

The 47-story Bell South Building dwarfs next to its neighbor. Only twenty years ago, Atlanta's skyscrapers were few. Surging business activity in the capital of the "New South" has vertically re-described the skyline.

▶ **Atlanta Aloft**

The built environment is never far from the natural in Atlanta. According to the U.S. Forest Service, the Atlanta metropolitan environs are the most heavily forested urban area in the country.

▲ Art in the Park

Verdant Piedmont Park inspires a noon-
time artist. A breathtaking public amenity,
"Atlanta's Common Ground" has enchant-
ed urban dwellers for over 100 years with
acres of in-town greens, walks, athletic
fields, and a large lake.

▶ Emerald City

Midtown seems miles away from the
respite of Piedmont Park just to the north.
Outdoor music festivals have offered
everything from the Atlanta Symphony
Orchestra to the Allman Brothers over
the years.

▲ Green Streets

Atlanta's tree-lined streets thread together
its myriad unique neighborhoods. Along
with the fabulous climate, shady tree
cover is a common element of residential
life here.

▶ Reflection

Burled roots and protective shade invite
lakeside readers and afternoon dreamers
to a quiet corner of Piedmont Park.
Readers of a local paper dubbed Piedmont
the "best place to play hookey."

▲ The Flair

Richard McDonald's sculpture—a gift to
Atlanta from the artist—celebrates the
passion of human endeavor and the pos-
sibilities of the human form. The sculpture toured the country in the "Flair
Across America" exhibition prior to the
centennial Olympiad in Atlanta.

▶ Pursuit of Excellence

The Georgia Dome, The Georgia World
Congress Center, and the Centennial
Olympic Park all converge on a 21-acre
campus revitalizing miles of formerly dilapi-
dated buildings. The Flair evokes a core
Atlanta theme—continual improvements
that push global frontiers for innovation.

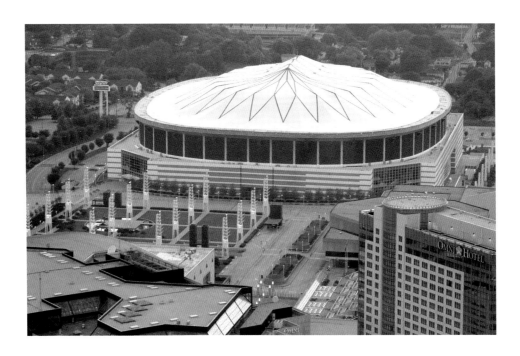

▲ The Georgia Dome

In taking the mantle from Athens for the centennial Olympiad, Atlanta prepared a fitting campus. The enormous nine acre enclosed arena is visible for miles with its teflon coated fiberglass roof. Home to the Atlanta Falcons and host to the 1996 Olympic Games, the Dome also offers concerts, World Supercross, monster truck rallies and even bullfighting!

▶ Arenas Abstract

Architectural elements from the Georgia Dome reflect in the glass of Philips Arena. Jorjorian's oeuvre captures Atlanta's fascination with the juxtaposition of the classical, the new and the abstract.

◀◀ Splendor in the Dark

The park at night beckons onlookers to fling off shoes and be part of the water and sound and color of the show. Bricks, music, lights and fountains represent earth, air, fire and water. The five rings represent the five major world regions; granite from each region is part of the park design.

▲ Wonder

A boy explores the pure interactivity of the Fountain of Rings.

▲ **Hydrodance**

Constantly changing patterns of water, sound, and light never cease to please.

▲ The Fabulous Fox

One of the largest movie palaces ever constructed, the Fox opened on Christmas Day 1929. The theatre's eclectic Islamic architectural references derive from the building's original purpose as a Shriner's Temple. High school students sparked the grassroots effort to restore the theatre and preserve it as a National Register Landmark in 1976.

▶ What'll Ya Have?

For a high-octane hot dog experience stop at the world's largest diner—the two-acre Varsity on North Avenue serving Georgia Tech and downtown. Pop inside to marvel over the ton of chopped onions, miles of hot dogs and 300 gallons of chili served daily. You'll hear only one refrain: dozens of counter hops barking "What'll Ya Have?" For curb service, use the drive-in. Nipsy Russell was once a car man at the V.

▶▶ Bright Future

A 123-foot tower near the Varsity pays homage to the Olympic Torch. Created by football star and designer Taz Anderson.

▲ The Gold Dome

The gilding with Georgia gold was added in 1957 to "make Georgia a shining example." Rumor has it that bits of gold can be found on the sidewalk after a hailstorm.

▶ Georgia State Capitol

In the reconstruction period, Georgia wanted to show a national sprit for "the capital of the New South," so it modeled its statehouse after the U.S. Capitol. The neo-classical Georgia State Capitol was completed in 1889 at a cost of almost a million dollars. Miss Freedom tops the dome with her light held high.

◀ The Big Chicken

Directions in Marietta are often given in
reference to the Big Chicken at the
Intersection of Highway 120 and U.S. 41.
This sheet-metal big bird is the hatchling
of entrepreneur Tubby Davis and engineer
Hubert Puckett. Applying a little Georgia
Tech ingenuity and good old Atlanta steel
to the problem of selling more fast food,
they created a 56-foot-tall landmark with
moving beak and rolling eyes—a cherished
piece of local kitsch since 1963.

▲ Catch the Blue Train

Atlanta's roots are in transport; the city
started as an antebellum railroad crossing
called Terminus. Now the MARTA train
provides rapid transit to city points ITP
(inside the perimeter) Interstates follow
the path of old rail beds.

▲ Nighthawks at the Diner

Ponce de Leon Avenue—locals just call it Ponce—bisects old Atlanta's north and south sides. The down, the out, and the up and up all come together on Ponce especially after last call. The Majestic has been serving round the clock diner fare since 1929 to a crowd more colorful than the neon.

▶ Wheels of Steel

A downtown DJ livens up the street spinning sound from his double decks.

LEFT LANE
BUSES AND
CAR POOLS
ONLY
UNLAWFUL TO
CROSS DOUBLE
SOLID WHITE
LINES
HOV
EXPRESS LANE
VIOLATORS
SUBJECT TO
FINES UP TO
$150

◀ The Big Peach

Saluting commercial growth and home-grown success stories from a landmark rooftop peach visible for miles at night.

▲ Road Atlanta

A section of traffic looks like a 16-lane raceway on a banked curve at midtown. Road Atlanta is actually northeast of the city near Lake Lanier, the home of regional, club, and world-level car and bike racing. Atlanta Motor Speedway south of town holds NASCAR and Legends racing.

▲ **World of Coke**

View the history of old Atlanta and the
future of the modern city all through a
Coke-themed lens! The World of Coke is
a three story interactive pavilion celebrat-
ing the city's fizziest business success.
The first Coca-Cola was poured at a soda
fountain near this site in 1886.

▲ **Heritage Steps**

Three centuries intersect at a Victorian landmark now dwarfed by surrounding Georgia State high-rises and Grady Memorial Hospital. Georgia State's Baptist Student Union uses the building today.

Rolling lawns and luxury homes define
the Paces Ferry Road area of Buckhead,
shades of a Tom Wolfe novel.

◀ Underground Atlanta

Underground Atlanta is a festival market-place and entertainment center designed by The Rouse Company, who worked with city planners to bring yet a new itera-tion to the oldest part of town at Alabama and Peachtree.

▲ Upstairs Downstairs

Venerable redevelopment gurus from Rouse company created a vibrant indoor–outdoor upstairs–downstairs des-tination that opened in 1989. Never still, the city may see another reinvention at Underground Atlanta—this time as a nighttime entertainment mecca open for business 'til 4 AM!

▲ Ground Zero

The Underground Atlanta attraction is near the zero milepost. The old freight depot and rail terminus was the epicenter of trade in antebellum Atlanta. The old rail beds, cobblestones, and gas lights from that era survived under new roads built above them after Sherman's fiery march.

▲ **Old Alabama**

Old Alabama Street, lined with shops and pushcarts, runs directly under upper Alabama Street in the underground market.

▶ **Bear on a Chain**

Transients, traders, con men and fortune hunters came through 19th century Atlanta's downtown market. Today a whimsical blend of sculpture and street vendors recreate the atmosphere.

◀ **On Any Sunday**

Public banners keep arts in the minds eye all week long. In a huge metropolitan area with dozens of art institutions and major universities, cultural activities flourish. There is never a dull weekend.

◀ ▲ **Peachtree Street**

One is hard pressed to find a peach tree growing in Atlanta but streets named Peachtree come a dime a dozen. There are now more than 50 streets containing the word Peachtree in addition to the main north-south thoroughfare linking downtown to Buckhead.

▲ East Atanta Evolving Hotspot

The new creative frontier for locals, East Atlanta is lower key and less touristy than Little Five Points a mile to the north. Like Broadway in New York and Peachtree in Atlanta its main drag (now Flat Shoals SE) is an ancient Native American trading path.

▶ Modern Times

Art, commerce and foliage join forces in reflective, amplified Atlanta fashion. Situated between the Hyatt Regency and the Coast States Insurance Building, Jerry Peart's "Grand Mercy" soars. The Hyatt is proud of its much imitated full story atrium and glass elevator; Peart's public work is the hotel's 1996 salute to the people of Atlanta.

▲ Hop that Train

Where? Marietta Square; only six blocks west of the Big Chicken!

▲ Marietta Down Under

Folks from the coast used to ride the train to the higher cooler ground in Marietta for the summer. The pecan meets the pasty at the Australian Bakery.

▲ **Southern Living**

Marietta Square boasts art, history, and leisure activities in the thick of a business hub. Antebellum homes around the square offer a taste of three centuries of Georgia life, mint julep style.

Downtown Rebirth

Sherman burned Atlanta in 1864 and the city has never looked back. Rising from the ashes stronger than ever, revitalization is in the city's genes. Cranes at work in the Centennial Park district are busy constructing new multi-use living quarters on a once-blighted area.

◀ **Sunwarmed Benches**

Take a break at Centennial Olympic Park. City sounds fade away; live oak fills the aromatic southern air.

▲ **Tribute**

An eight-ton bronze commemorating the Olympic legacy. The three runners represent the first games (776 BC), the first modern games (1896) and the Atlanta centennial games in 1996. The stones at the base are a gift from the Ancient City of Olympia to the people of Atlanta.

▲ **Cotton Mill Details**

A glimpse at industrial roots near
Cabbagetown, a neighborhood near
Oakland Cemetery built to house cotton
mill workers.

▲ **Carter Center**

The nonprofit academic research center is located on the site of the Battle of Atlanta. President and Mrs. Jimmy Carter rededicated the grounds to serve their founding mission: advancing peace and health through work on conflict resolution and human rights. President Carter's library and museum are housed on the campus.

◀ **Inside CNN Center**

The global headquarters of Turner Broadcasting is also home to shops, eateries and convention hotels. CNN's revolutionary 24 hour news concept is an icon of the new south's innovative business ethos.

▲ **Kriegshaber House**

One of the last grand Victorian mansions standing, this house connects Little Five Points with Inman Park. Victor Hugo Kriegshaber was an Atlanta businessman, philanthropist, and civic leader.

⌃ Cyclorama at Grant Park

"The Battle of Atlanta" is a huge circular painting and diorama from the 19th century depicting the local Civil War campaign. It is also the best way to learn the geography of Atlanta. From a revolving stage, see Kennesaw Mountain to the West, Stone Mountain to the East, and the train beds and foot-tracks that form toda's major arteries.

▲ A Cannon Bears Witness

Fierce fighting broke out at Kennesaw Battlefield between June 18th and July 3rd, 1864. The Atlanta Campaign claimed or wounded over 67,000 soldiers.

▶ Birds of a Feather

Known to frequent flyers as ATL for Hartsfield-Jackson International Airport, the metro area also offers over 10 regional airports helping private aviators arrive closer to their ultimate destination.

The Dream Lives On

The first stop on a freedom trail pilgrimage is the Martin Luther King, Jr. National Historic Site visitor's center. Exhibits focus on Dr. King, leadership, and the struggle for civil rights. Peace Plaza is in the foreground.

▲ Ebenezer Baptist Church

A heritage sanctuary founded only nine years after reconstruction. Rev. Martin Luther King, Sr. delivered his message of non-violence and equality here for 44 years. His famous son served as co-pastor from 1960 until 1968. The landmark Gothic Revival church is undergoing a multi-million dollar restoration.

▲ **Fire Station No. 6**

This fire house served the Sweet Auburn neighborhood of Martin Luther King's boyhood for 97 years. It now houses fire engine memorabilia and a bookstore for African-American history and culture.

▲ **Speaking Truth to Power**

"I refuse to accept the view… that the bright daybreak of peace and brotherhood can never become a reality."
—Dr. Martin Luther King, Jr.

▶ **Birthplace of a King**

501 Auburn Avenue—the Queen Anne style home of young "M.L." King until 1941. His home life bustled with family, grandparents and boarders. Ebenezer Baptist Church is just down the street.

▶ Meditative Memorial

Resting in view of Ebenezer Baptist
Church and the King Center, America's
greatest crusader for social justice is "free
at last" at the reflecting pool of the Martin
Luther King, Jr. Center for Nonviolent
Social Change.

▲ **Porch Life on Moreland**

Vernacular bungalows on Moreland
Avenue are representative of the larger
Inman Park-Moreland Historic District des-
ignated by the Department of the Interior.

▲ Home of the Braves

Turner Field opened for baseball in April, 1997. It was retrofitted from Olympic Stadium as a high technology ballpark with gigantic dual video boards and 59 luxury suites.

◀ **The Georgia Peach**

Ty Cobb slides into base outside Turner Field. His 1929 career record of 4,191 hits held until Pete Rose topped it.

▲ **Lefty**

Southpaw great Warren Spahn cast in his signature high kick pitching style outside Turner Field.

▲ **Curve Balls**

Whimsical giant baseballs line the
entranceway outside the Plaza at Turner
Field. Ballpark meets theme park in this
state-of-the-art entertainment complex.

▲ **Abstracts**

High style lights the way in Buckhead, the
Beverly Hills of the South.

Callanwolde Fine Arts Center

New York architect Henry Horbostel—
designer of the Emory University campus—
created Gothic-Tudor "Callanwolde" for
Charles Howard Candler. The Candler family
founded the Coca-Cola Company; the estate
is named for their Irish forbearers' Callan
Castle. Naturalized gardens of azalea, dogwood, weeping cherry, and crabapple have
been carefully restored by the Dekalb
County Federation of Garden Clubs.

◀ R. Thomas Deluxe Diner

R. Thomas is a wacky one-of-a-kind all
hours diner sandwiched between midtown and Buckhead on Peachtree Street.
The Food Network has chronicled the
eclectic fare and décor: health food, com-
fort food, live birds, talking parrots, and a
carved sculpture garden.

▲ Liberty…en route from Key West

Things get weirder after dark when hard-par-
tying Buckhead nighthawks roll in to refuel
on R. Thomas food and juices. An in-house
psychic and other eccentrics hold court in
the wee hours. Legend has it that the owner
lost his keys on opening night in 1985 so he
kept the place open ever since.

▲ The Junkman's Daughter

An East Village boutique with big box pro-
portions in Little Five Points. Junkman's is
10,000 square foot purveyor of hip para-
phernalia, funky vintage outfits, goth gear,
and club clothes. Cool cheap shoes are a
signature line.

▲ Variety Playhouse

Little Five Points is the place for inde-
pendent music: live, street, recorded, you
name it. Record shops offer broad cere-
bral inventory. The Variety is a 1940's
movie house reborn as a performance
venue with national bookings.

▲ **Attitude**

The Vortex is a burger restaurant with a
façade that's right at home among Little
Five Points merchants.

▲ It's not Tara…

….although Gone with the Wind was indeed written here. The wide porch with crisp white rockers and rails hint at the sweet magnolia and lemonade pace of plantation life. The Margaret Mitchell Home has been surrounded by a busy commercial district since the close of World War I.

▶ Margaret Mitchell Home

A phoenix just like the city around it, the Mitchell home has endured several rounds of fire and restoration. It is now part of the Atlanta History Center. Mitchell lived in the 10-unit building then known as the Crescent Apartments when she wrote her novel. She called it "The Dump," but friends flocked to her bohemian literary salon in Apt #1.

The Garden Suburb

Inman Park was one of the first planned and designed "garden suburbs" of the style pioneered by Frederick Law Olmstead. It was highly fashionable when developed after reconstruction and into the early 20th century. The community is now a revitalized in-town neighborhood and National Register Historic District.

▲ **Shotgun Houses in Sweet Auburn**

Sweet Auburn is the soul of America. In the years after the Civil War, entrepreneurial African-Americans settled here, built homes, and established businesses. In it's heyday over 100 black owned or operated businesses lined the tony Auburn Avenue district. In the 1950s and 1960s the civil rights movement centered here.

▲ **Inman Park**

The blossoming streetscapes of Inman Park's Victorians, Bungalows, and Craftsman style dwellings are just part of the traditional neighborhood charm. Human scale, proximity to downtown, and a cohesive sense of community are perks of in-town living.

▲ Virginia–Highlands

The charm of Virginia-Highlands is the mix of turn of the century bungalows, progressive cuisine, and unique home and garden shops. Highland Hardware—a splendid toy store for woodworkers—is standing room only on Father's Day!

▶ Esprit de Corps

Fire Station No. 19 in Virginia-Highlands was built in 1925. Always in top condition and ready to serve, this station utilized the first motorized equipment in Atlanta. Today firemen from No. 19 advocate for cutting edge GIS units.

▲ **March to the Sea**

More than 17,0000 Union soldiers felled
in Georgia are buried at Marietta National
Cemetery. Southern casualties lie separat-
ed in Marietta Confederate Cemetery.

▲ **Brothers**

"…We cannot hallow this ground. The brave men, living and dead who struggled here have consecrated it far above our poor power to add or detract."

–Abraham Lincoln

▲ **The Governor's Mansion, Buckhead**

Seven governors have taken residence here: Lester Maddox, Jimmy Carter, George Busbee, Joe Frank Harris, Zell Miller, Roy Barnes, and Sonny Perdue. The commodious home includes a ball-room for 150 and a presidential suite.

▲ **Inside the Governor's Mansion**

One of the finest collections of Federal period furnishings is housed in the State of Georgia's Tuxedo Park mansion. The first floor is used for entertaining.

96

◀ The Winding Stair

A magnificent interior reminiscent of a seashell spirals in a delightful sweep to the Governor's second floor living quarters.

▲ Attentive

Doric columns add formality and order to the entrance at the Governor's Mansion on West Paces Ferry Road. True to Atlanta's spirit of revival and growth, the 1967 mansion replaces Woodhaven, a privately owned Tudor residence on the site.

Serene Neighborhood

Lush green lawns carpet a row of brick homes in suburban Atlanta.

▲ Outwitting the Traffic

Downtown is more enjoyable if you know how to maneuver. With headphones and a bicycle, no amount of traffic can spoil a midday break.

▶ Five Points

Five Points anchors downtown at the convergence of Marietta, Edgewood, Decatur, Peachtree NE and Peachtree SW. The area is being re-imagined as one of the world's great livable city centers capitalizing on existing pedestrian friendly café-lined walkways.

•BREAKFAST
• PHILLY STEAKS
•SALADS - GYROS
• BURGERS - YOGURT
Chicken Fillet
Hot Wings
Reuben
Salads
Garden Burger
rozen Yogurt

▲ Destination Buckhead

The Atlanta Journal-Constitution calls Buckhead the place where "old money lives and new money parties." Distinctive shopping and saucy nightlife attract visitors from all over the country.

▶ The Georgian Terrace Hotel

Floodlights accentuate the dramatic curved brick and marble elegance of the landmark Fox Theatre District hotel at Peachtree and Ponce de Leon.

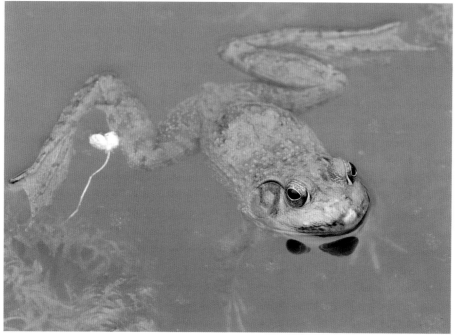

▲ Handsome Prince?

The Atlanta Botanical Gardens includes fabulous water lily gardens with their own watchful sentinels.

▶ Urban Eden

Walking trails wind from garden to conservatory to wooded glen at the 15-acre botanical gardens adjacent to Piedmont Park. Sculpture, water features and plenty of spots to refresh the senses are carefully sited among the specimen plants.

▲ Mountain Laurel

Atlanta's famous tree canopy is layered. Much of the beauty lies in fragrant understory plants with massive blooms: mountain laurel, dogwood, azaleas and vibernum.

▶ Skyward Stretch

A realm guided by the senses. Each corner of the gardens offers a quiet delight.

▲ Beckoning

The closer you get, the more complex the scenery!

▶ Chorus of Orchids

Gorgeous orchids dazzle visitors at Fuqua Orchid Center. The facility houses extensive orchid collections from tropical lowlands and upland environments.

▲ Bowing to the Center

Botanicals reveal their abstract splendor.

▶ Armed to the Teeth

Gardens under glass are arranged by environment, from dry desert heat to highly humid forest. State of the art computer systems monitor the conservatories. The botanical gardens are a manifestation of Atlanta's commercial success. Generous endowments from local business leaders funded the rapid rise of this young—yet globally acclaimed—institution.

▲ **Trust us; we won't bite?**

The carnivorous Venus fly trap (Dionaea muscipula) is a centerpiece of morbid fascination for garden visitors. The clam hinged flowers snap shut around unsuspecting prey.

▶ **Innocents Abroad**

Unsuspecting insects enter the funnel like pitcher plant whose sweet nectar belies carnivorous intent. Unlike the fly-trap, pitcher plants use a passive mechanism to attract their meals.

▲ New Beginnings

A bit of snakeskin is the only trace of a reptile's fresh start downstream. Scary to some, the presence of snakes indicates a healthy watershed.

▶ Chattahoochee Dreamin'

"It's a rare occasion when within the city limits of one of our major cities, one can find pure water and trout and free canoe-ing and rapids and the seclusion of the Earth the way God made it. But the Chattahoochee River is this kind of place."
—President Jimmy Carter
August 15, 1978

▲ Fly Fishing on the Chattahoochee

Year round fishing is available with 23 species of game fish on 48 miles of protected national recreation area. What more could anglers wish for?

▶ Canadian Tourist

Migratory birds don't usually head for the city, but the 4200 acres of Chattahoochee preserve offer a wilderness stopover in the midst of urbanity for seasoned travelers like the Canada goose.

▲ **Meanering by the Mountain**

A landmark for 300 million years, Stone
Mountain is one of the largest granite out-
croppings in the Eastern United States.
Part natural wonder, part recreational facility and part theme park, one can ride,
bike, or hike in over 3,000 acres 16 miles
east of downtown Atlanta.

▲ **Stonewall on Stone Wall**

Cable car riders en route to the bald
mountaintop get a close-up view of the
enormous wall carving depicting three
Confederate heroes: President Jefferson
Davis and Generals Robert E. Lee and
Thomas J. "Stonewall" Jackson. Jackson
was named for the "wall of stone" stance
his troops maintained on the battlefield at
First Manassas.

▲ ▶ **Creative Loaf**

Voted best place to watch the sunrise and
sunset by Creative Loafing readers. Stone
Mountain rises in stark contrast to its
tranquil moat-like surroundings like a
mammoth granite artisanal bread.

▲ Grant Park

Rustic signs throughout the city designate
public parks and attractions where the air
is filled with the scent of Georgia oak. A
recreational counterpoint to Atlanta's
modernity, the park system provides acres
of accessible public greenspaces. Excellent
well located parks truly measure a city's
greatness and beauty.

▶ Wise Eye

Zoo Atlanta has three female elephants,
including Starlet O'Hara. The elephants
are right at home in their Georgia red clay
habitat—Mzima Springs in Africa is also a
red clay environment.

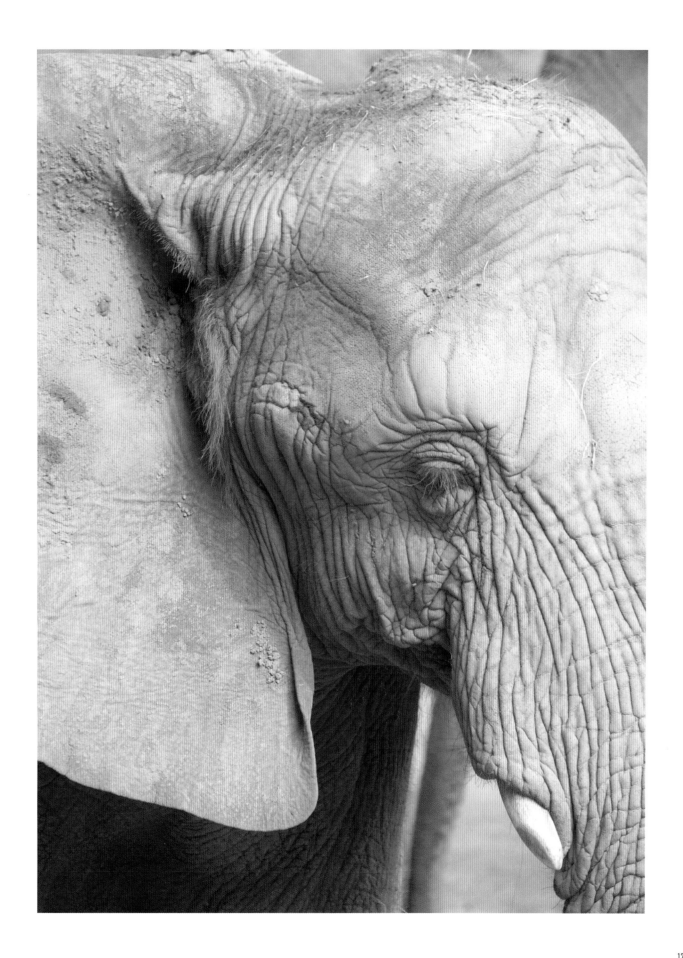

▲ ▶ **Color and Texture**

From flamingoes and peacocks to the massive rhinoceros, Zoo Atlanta is home to an array of colorful birds and impressive animals.

▲ **Much to Ponder**

The Sumatran orangutans at Zoo Atlanta
enjoy an Indonesian rain forest habitat
created for them in Grant Park.
Sumatrans sport bright orange fur and are
the world's largest tree dwellers. Several
young have been born at the zoo—a vital
beginning in the fight against endanger-
ment.

Baby otters in leisurely communication take advantage of Zoo Atlanta's wetlands. Otters are highly intelligent marine mammals; they are able to use rocks as tools!

About the Author

Priscilla Morris lived in Atlanta during the
millennial technology boom and spends
time with her family in the area whenever
she can. A freelance writer, she is active in
community development and historic
preservation. She loves the small details
that give an area its sense of place. She is
a member of the Urban Land Institute and
the Project for Public Spaces. Currently
she is involved in mounting a large public
sculpture commemorating Frederick
Douglass. Her previous work for Twin
Lights Publishers is *Maryland's Eastern
Shore: A Photographic Portrait.*